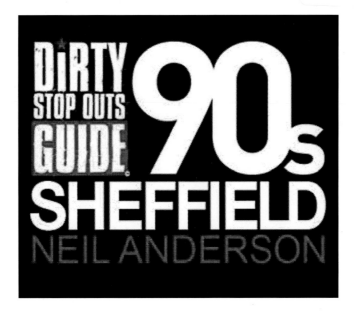

Published by

The original trio behind Viva Salsa! club night; (left to right) Tony Dente, Adrian Bagnoli and Gian Bohan

Published by ACM Retro Ltd,
51 Clarkegrove Road
Sheffield
S10 2NH

Visit ACM Retro at: www.acmretro.com

Neil Anderson asserts the moral right to be identified as the author of this work.
A catalogue record for this book is available from the British Library.

**Though much of the 1990s were quiet on the protest front when you
compare it to the 1980s, we were out in force to say 'no' to the Poll Tax**

Dirty Stop Out's - the first ever photo shoot for the original publication in 1995

Herol 'Bomber' Graham impresses school pupils with his skipping prowess

C☺NTENTS

Sheffield Lord Mayor Peter Price never seemed to be away from nightclubs on his watch - here he is helping launch the Roundhouse under Ponds Forge

**Leadmill staff gearing up for a hectic and very
successful decade in the 1990s**

Security outside Carver Street's Orchis

STOP OUT AND STAY OUT

The former Adelphi cinema in Attercliffe was one of many historic buildings that was given a new lease of life as a nightclub

It was way back in early 1995 when I started mulling over plans for the first ever 'Dirty Stop Out's Guide to Sheffield'.

I'd already had pretty good indoctrination to the workings of the after dark scene thanks to time spent at Sheffield City Hall and being a part of Radio One's Sound City visit in 1993.

But I never dreamt that 'Dirty Stop Out's' would still be around and part of my life nearly two decades later.

At the time I was on a temporary contract, working in public relations at Sheffield Town Hall. It was a colleague who suggested I write a guide to nightclubs as part of a wider campaign to put nightlife back on the agenda and help persuade licensing magistrates to give out new licences.

We both agreed, if the plan got the go-ahead, the council would have little choice but to keep me on for a while to ensure it was finished.

It worked. In fact it helped keep me there for nigh on five years before I left for pastures new.

I came up with a few suggested names for the publication. 'Dirty Stop Out's Guide' was on my list but the least favoured as far as I was concerned. But everyone I spoke to loved it, so that's how it came about.

The more research I did into Sheffield's after dark

experience, the more I realised there was far more going on than people assumed. It started to dawn on me that the publication could be a real eye opener and help market a far more vibrant scene than many realised existed.

I'd regularly visit four or five nightclubs on any given Saturday night under the moniker of 'research'. Sundays would be total write off.

The reaction to the first 'Dirty Stop Outs Guide to Sheffield' was truly amazing. Everyone seemed to want a copy. I suddenly found myself as the city's spokesperson on nightlife and clubbing, not bad for someone that would normally feel more at home in a sweaty punk hangout.

A coach was duly hired to launch the publication. It took 40-odd journalists for a Saturday night club-crawl so they could sample the city's nightlife. We lost nearly half of them en route but the things they said about the city's nightlife was fantastic.

Looking back, there's little doubt the late nineties scene was about as good as it got for Sheffield; it was ranked as one of the top night's out in the country.

The pace of change was phenomenal once the licensing magistrates had relented and started giving new licences out.

In the early 1990s we were losing Sheffield audiences to other cities, by the mid-1990s the situation had turned full circle and we were the place to be.

The one thing we had above all others was the strength of our independent operators and club promoters.

Hotels were sold out every weekend and admission charges in some dance venues were going through the roof (but they were still selling out).

From 1995 onwards there seemed to be new venues opening virtually every week.

Many cite the 1990s as a fusion of every type of youth cult that had gone on for decades before - it was an era built on recycling and rip-offs.

But did anyone care? No, we were too busy enjoying ourselves.

Britpop dominated the charts and Oasis shamelessly recycled the Beatles with devastating effect.

In many respects it was an era when left field was accepted as mainstream - more than helped by New Labour coining the 'Cool Britannia' phrase and Tony Blair inviting the Gallagher's and friends for drinks at Number 10 after Labour's 1997 landslide victory.

Boy bands were knocked from the number one spot by upstarts like Blur; a new breed of comedy entered the ring led by Reeves and Mortimer and mouthy artists like Damien Hirst and Tracey Emin became millionaires.

Unlike the 1980s, the 1990s were much less reliant on the USA for influence. So much of it was home-grown and the county oozed confidence. We were even, for a few months at least, proud of the Spice Girls.

The biggest cultural contributions from over the water as far as the youth were concerned were probably 'Friends' and Alanis Morrisette's 'Jagged Little Pill' album which seem to top the charts forever.

John Cooper said: "Main thing I remember about the 1990s is everyone, and I mean everyone, wanting a mobile phone. They were such a 'must have' item and I don't think 'pay as you go' had even been invented then."

Whilst the dance clubs bred a generation of image conscious clubbers, the rise of karaoke rewrote the style book in many quarters of the city

Reopening Kikis as the Havana influenced Rhythm Room was a brave attempt to cash in on the after work market - sadly it wasn't to last

The Forum shopping complex and cafe bar was a major success throughout the decade - and continues to lead on trends to this day

Club nights were seen as a new income stream for Sheffield City Hall as promoters queued up to hire its ballroom - Robbie Bifield and colleagues did their utmost to keep the house in order when the masses arrived every Friday and Saturday night

The sheer weight of numbers that started arriving in Sheffield every weekend from the mid-1990s onwards was a massive boost for local hotels - here's the host of one settling down to a good read

SHEFFIELD PARTY CENTRAL

CHAPTER ONE

Bikinis were the weapon of choice for many females of the dance persuasion

The mere thought of New York clubbers making a beeline for 21st century Sheffield would be laughed off the dance floor, but 15 years ago it was a reality.

Steel City was renowned as an after dark tour de force and UK cities were queuing up to follow its example.

The pace of the rise and fall of Sheffield as a nationally renowned party city was quite incredible.

Fortunes were made and lost (mostly lost) seemingly overnight and at one point it seemed every disused building in the city centre was being eyed as a potential nightclub or bar.

One venue that really came into its own in the era was

the City Hall Ballroom. The scramble to book club nights in there was relentless. Brighton Beach, Hotpants, Drop - everyone seemed to want to entertain their audiences in the historic space that originally opened in 1932.

Former banks, building societies, shops, leisure centres - everything was fair game in the over arching rush to open a venue.

And when space was running out in the city centre, eyes drifted down the East End to Attercliffe and the shiny new Valley Centertainment area.

The era certainly didn't start that way.

Clubland in the early 1990s was a bit of disaster area.

The licensing magistrates,

in their infinite wisdom, hadn't handed out a new nightclub licence for years and flatly turned down one for the £1.4m 'style club' project (later to be unveiled as The Republic).

It took the venue three years to finally win their case.

Though the club ended up going bust within months of opening, it helped instil a

sea change in the attitudes of the magistrates ; they took a step back and started leaving it up to the market to decide when there were enough bars and clubs in Sheffield, rather than simply refusing new ventures out of hand.

It quickly became open season for would-be venue owners.

New life was suddenly coursing through the veins of Attercliffe's then derelict Adelphi Cinema as it opened as a nightclub; a former suit outlet opened as Capitol club on Matilda Street; Ponds Forge sports centre threw its own clubland hat into the ring with The Roundhouse and the cavernous Pulse and Vogue and Club Wow opened in the shadow of Sheffield Arena as investors decided 'out-of-town clubbing' was the way forward and backed the Valley Centertainment area.

All-night venue Niche gave clubbers every excuse never to go home whilst Gatecrasher - the organisation that moved into the former Republic - became a global clubland powerhouse.

Sheffield seemed almost blessed with a cultural Midas Touch while London looked on dumbfounded as we landed the multi-million pound funding for our very own National Centre for Popular Music and Jarvis Cocker's immortal 'Sorted For Es and Whizz' line became the buzz phrase for an entire generation.

Culinary sophistication largely stayed away from the city centre for the majority of the 1990s - you had to go to the suburbs for that - and it wasn't until after the Millennium that decent restaurants started popping up in great numbers.

Clubbers were more than happy with the marvellous Pepe's on Cambridge Street which served coffee and pizza all night or Greasy Vera's mobile catering.

We also lost the alcohol-infused carnage of the Pyjama Jump; The student fundraiser that turned much of the city centre into a marauding cross-dressing party zone of almost mythical proportions.

The gay scene tried and failed to make an impact in the city centre and had more success in Attercliffe.

Paul Smith said: "The party scene in Sheffield in the late 1990s was absolutely phenomenal. There was little to touch it. There was so much happening. It was such a cool time to be in the city. Who could forget amazing nights like Trash and Viva Salsa? There really was such a great mix."

Today there's little left of the clubland renaissance. The Roundhouse is a fitness suite; Pulse and Vogue was sold off as office space; Club Wow is a kids' play centre; the Music Factory is now Sainsbury's and Gatecrasher burned

down.

Licensing deregulation signalled the death knell for many nightclubs as bars were given late licenses and allowed to set up in direct competition. DJing was also losing its attraction as rock music returned to prominence towards the end of the decade.

But, to many, the 1990s Sheffield club scene was the absolute zenith of after dark action that successfully attracted punters from the four corners of the country. The party was only punctuated by a week or two in Ibiza every year for many.

Danny Clark said: "Sheffield was a true party land capital in the nineties - it was absolutely amazing".

These days the tide has seemingly turned against the clubbing generation. Even Gatecrasher, who were looking to move back into the city centre, were given short shrift by the powers that be, in 2010.

Raising a glass to 'Choices' leisure card in Sheffield

Pole dancing was sweeping the nation by the late 1990s - the first venue to open in Sheffield was the Dancing Dollar in Attercliffe

The men behind the opening of the popular Unit nightclub which, in more recent times, is now known as Corporation rock club

Lord Mayor of Sheffield Peter Price celebrated his year in office with the 'Rock 'n' Drop' night at Sheffield City Hall Ballroom

Belly dancing was a popular way to fitness

☺Going out in the nineties...

Richard Abbey said: "Given my tender years (!), my experience of the nineties was more or less 1995 onwards. At that time it was still very much pub and then club, there were no 'late bars' in those days.

"Nights out with college friends usually involved getting the 120 in to town so you could use your bus ticket for Berlins (two Lamot Pils for £1?).

My main memories of Berlins revolve around would we get in or not? If not we used to walk around the block for 10 minutes and then go back hoping the bouncers wouldn't remember you. It was always heaving inside. The drinks were crap and you usually drank whatever came up on the 'wheel' (was it the 'Don't Forget Your Toothbrush' theme music), usually the aforementioned Lamot Pils, Diamond White or vodka and something insignificant.

"After Berlins it was either on to Roxy, Uropa (I missed Isabella's by a few months) or Capitol, which is now Plug.

"Roxy I just remember being huge, you could get lost in there. There was even a café upstairs. The dress code was pretty strict too - no jeans! Definitely one for the townies!

"Uropa was pretty forgettable but Capitol was the one that really sticks in my mind and was probably where I first discovered house music. It was dark, dingy, smoky and had sloping toilets, go-go dancers above the bar and more than its fair share of unsavoury characters, but the music was great.

"I remember going there for my 18th birthday. It was January and snowing but we went anyway, not really thinking about the consequences. When we left the club around 2am (last bus anyone?) Arundel Gate was about a foot deep in snow, there were no buses, no taxis, nothing - and my friend and I didn't have coats on, just the usual YSL shirt and pinstripe trouser combo.

"Thinking we might stand a better chance of getting a taxi or a bus near the train station we headed there. Luckily there were a few taxis - and plenty of people waiting for them - but when asked where we were going (Mosborough), we were told 'no chance'.

"There was only one thing to do which was find a phone box - no mobiles then - and phone my dad. He said he'd come and get us. We said we'd start walking and we'd be home before we knew it. Unfortunately, he drove down the Parkway (several times he told us) while we walked up through Wybourn and the Manor. By chance, and seeing the oasis of lights of the Esso petrol station on Prince of Wales Road, we headed there for a warm and maybe another phone call. Lo and behold, my dad was there and was greeted by two 18 year olds whose shirts were frozen stiff with frost and had about six inches of snow on top of their heads, resembling 'Kid 'n' Play'.

"It was still a good night though and we still talk about it now!"

"The Republic offered something completely different. It had a completely different feel to any other club I'd ever been to, I'm not quite sure why. Maybe it was the layout, with its different level dance floors, walkways, balconies etc or maybe it was just the music. Disco 2000 was a favourite on Thursdays but the Musiquarium nights on Saturday were really good - I can remember queuing round the block to get in. I think in that late nineties period, and before Gatecrasher took over, I probably saw some of the best house DJs of the time without ever really knowing it.

"It was from there that I started going to Gatecrasher and then moved onto the Unit on Corporation Street before things started getting too crazy.

"Pubs that we went too during that mid to late-nineties period pretty much revolved around how we got into town. If we went by bus it was the Yorkshire Grey, Berlins and that end of town. If we went by tram, it was the Stonehouse, Dikkins, Yates... all the really terrible places looking back now."

HELL HATH NO FURY LIKE THE MEADOWHELL EFFECT ON THE CITY CENTRE

CHAPTER TWO

The rush to get in Meadowhall on the day it opened

Sheffield made some bold moves to re-establish an economic base following the decimation of its heavy industry in the 1980s.

Nothing was bigger, or more controversial depending on who you talk to, than the transformation of its East End.

September 4, 1990, will be a date firmly etched in the memories of scores of Sheffield and Rotherham retailers as their takings fell off a cliff with the opening of Meadowhall shopping centre.

Manchester city centre might be able to co-exist with the nearby out-of-town Trafford Centre - the same didn't happen here.

Meadowhall was a hit with the public from the day it opened - 280 shops appealing to all pockets; from the downmarket at one end to the aspirational at the other, with free parking for thousands of cars.

Sheffield city centre didn't stand a chance. It was a far cry from the all-conquering retail offering of the early seventies that would attract shoppers from right around the region. It's only now, 23 years later, that the multi-million pound regeneration of The Moor and the re-siting of Sheffield Markets is giving real impetus to the city centre once again.

Meadowhall attracted nearly 20 million visitors in its first year. It even had its own in-house TV studio in the sprawling Oasis food hall.

Many tried to shun it and gave it the tag 'Meadowhell' but they were definitely in a minority.

Chris Twiby said: "Sheffield city centre really didn't stand a chance. Meadowhall offered the two things it didn't - 12,000 free car parking spaces and, once you got inside, good weather. And that's before you started on the quality of the shops,

DiRTY STOP OUTS .COM

cleanliness and catering. Even the one good thing Sheffield city centre did have, in the shape of the really good food court inside Orchard Square, was turned into a shop."

But there were other areas of economic diversity championed by the Town Hall that were rather kinder to the evening economy in the 1990s.

The main one was the Cultural Industries Quarter, an area of the city centre given over to 'creative industries'.

Now things didn't come more creative than music and clubbing and associated businesses and individuals were welcomed with open arms.

Cornerstones of the Cultural Industries Quarter were the Leadmill

nightclub and Red Tape Studios, two institutions that, though they had established themselves in the 1980s, would truly find their calling in the 1990s.

They were joined in the era by the Showroom Cinema, the groundbreaking Republic nightclub (more of that later), Niche and the comings and goings of various recording studios.

But everything, as far as the Cultural Industries Quarter was concerned, was lining up for the icing on the cake - the opening of the National Centre for Popular Music; the Lottery funded attraction that was lined up to be the catalyst for the next multi-million phase of development for the area.

The Leadmill cafe

Sixties icon Frank White was just as popular in the '90s

Steve Bush remembers a particular trip to the Pheasant Inn, Sheffield Lane Top.

He said: "In the mid 1990s, I was back in Sheffield, after spending twenty years travelling the world. "I'd made lots of good friends on the way, and one especially, who like me was called Steve, became a friend for life. We shared a love of good beer, hot curry and live rock music, which continues to today.

"Steve and his wife Sue were coming up from their home in Grantham to stay for a long weekend and Steve had said that he'd like to see some live music, so trawling through the Sheffield Telegraph, I found that one of my old haunts, The Pheasant at Sheffield Lane Top, was still putting on regular shows, and this Friday Frank White would be playing. I remembered watching Frank on many occasions before I left home, and knew that he always put on a good show, so I dug out my bus timetable and we jumped on a number 47 for the journey across town.

"As we made our way into the concert room I was mildly surprised to see Frank himself collecting the gate money, £3. "Still, I smiled inwardly, doing things on a tight budget. I ordered a couple of pints of John Smiths and we carried them through a smoky haze over to a table in the corner, the sticky carpet causing my tread to falter slightly. Although I hadn't been here since the mid '70s, (Sunday night disco with topless go-go girls shaking to Santana's 'Soul Sacrifice') it seemed little had changed. "There were some great pictures on the wall, a blow up of the "With The Beatles" sleeve photo, Hendrix, Marley and a handful

of other rock icons. On the next table sat Phil Johnson, a friend from the old days and Stones enthusiast (the band, not the beer) who had himself played the clubs in a few R'n'B groups. "We shook hands and he joined us at our table. Reminiscing our Parson Cross childhoods we were well into our third pint before Frank and the band came on stage. I was not really sure what to expect but when they went into the opening bars of 'Lawdy Miss Clawdy' I just knew we were in for a great evening. "Frank's power chord licks and his throaty blues voice were perfect for this old Lloyd Price number, and on this occasion he was well supported by his son Joel on Hammond Organ

and a big guy called Jeremy who played a massive six string bass but threw it about like a ukulele. "The drummer was of the same vintage as Frank but I never got his name. As he finished, the small but enthusiastic crowd cheered and hollered and Frank took no time at all before going into a frenetic version of 'Mohair Sam'. The first half dozen numbers continued at a hectic pace and included a good few R'n'R standards like 'Blue Moon of Kentucky' and 'Money Honey' with the atmosphere becoming electric, before they decided to slow things down a bit with a song about the Louisiana floods of the 20s followed by a slow homage to Elvis - 'Tupelo'. As Frank announced a short break I remember taking a deep breath

Frank White flanked by a pair of Steves

Frank on stage

and thinking that this was indeed something special.

"Chatting during the break, my mate Steve was gushing in his praise for the band, and having run out of superlatives he just kept shaking his head and murmuring "Brilliant - Absolutely Brilliant!" The place was full by now, and I had to push through a throng at the bar to get served. I replenished our beer glasses and sat back down in anticipation, and there was passionate applause as the guys came back on stage to take up their positions. They began with a Ray Charles song, 'Tell me what I say' which allowed Joel to show his prowess on The Hammond, and some prowess it was too! "He used the full extent of all the unique Hammond intricacies, and a loud cheer went up as he finished his solo. Next came a great range of songs including a great cover of Chuck Berry's 'Johnny B Goode' complete with Hendrix style middle third, and Buddy Holly's 'Not Fade Away'. "I really thought that from here on it couldn't get much better, but I was to be proven wrong. Firstly Frank went almost solo on Dobie Gray's 'Drift Away', lending a beautiful subtlety to a haunting chorus, and came close to letting the crowd join in. "He then rattled out the opening bars to 'On Broadway' This was the real high spot of the night. Covered by many artists, this song about thwarted ambitions is always a real show stopper, but tonight Frank played as though his life depended on it. "His face contorted as he bent the high strings to force out a glorious solo, never missing a beat of the chords. Joel and Jeremy kept the rhythms solid, each enjoying a short burst of the limelight, before Frank came back and tore the place apart with his final solo. As it drew to a close both band and audience were shattered and it felt as though I'd been through the spin cycle on a Hotpoint front loader! "Everyone took a breather as Joel and his dad had a quick chat about how to close the show, before the instantly recognisable "Sunshine Of Your Love" leapt out of Frank's bottle-green Strat and we all smiled in wonderment as they brought the show to its superb conclusion.

"There would be no encore.

"There was nothing left to give.

"As Steve and I walked down Barnsley Rd, flagging down anything that remotely resembled a cab, we chatted excitedly about the performance we'd witnessed and ran through our respective mental diaries to see when we could do it again. "We were to come back to The Pheasant and watch Frank and his constantly changing line up, many times throughout that decade. We also travelled to see him, wandering as far afield as Wigan, and were never disappointed. Always exciting, often unpredictable and occasionally brilliant, it was our favourite Friday night out, and, by a mile, the best three quidsworth in town!"

The launch of Supertram

The installation was a bugbear for the entire city in the 1990s - here's High Street

Celebrating the World Student Games at Don Valley Stadium

Ray Gridley, director of the World Student Games

Poll Tax protestors in Sheffield

THE REPUBLIC CHANGED THE COURSE OF NIGHTLIFE HISTORY IN SHEFFIELD

CHAPTER THREE

Dressed to kill

No venue defined the growing confidence in Sheffield's evening economy better than the Republic.

Though its life was a rollercoaster from beginning to end, the significance of what it achieved was pivotal for the growth and profile of the evening economy for the rest of the decade.

If there'd been no Republic you wonder how the fortunes of the city's nightlife would have fared.

Its transformation of the former Roper and Wreaks steelworks into a state-of-the-art nightclub was truly breathtaking.

The £1.4million scheme to get the place up and running lasted nearly three years, with a long running battle to try and get a licence being played out in the press.

The original plan was for the 1,200 capacity venue to be far more than your average nightclub - and initially it was.

The drinks licence was finally granted at Sheffield Crown Court by Judge Tom Cracknell, who overturned a previous ruling. The Republic was the city's first new nightclub in over 12 years.

Five young entrepreneurs were behind the project: Anwar Akhtar, Neil Midgley, Jerome Curran, Tony Fitzgerald and Fran Hilbert.

Anwar Akhtar and Jerome Curran first came to Sheffield as students and started promoting club nights in the late 1980s at the then Locarno (later to be renamed the Palais, then Music Factory and then, at the end

of the decade, BED). They started with student night, 'Blow Out', which regularly attracted over 1,000 on a Thursday night.

In 1990 they set up Die Hard Promotions (later to become Grade Trade Ltd) which eventually took over promotion of the entire roster of club nights at the Palais.

Anwar Akhtar said of the granting of the licence for the Republic: "It is going to put Sheffield on the map. It will take Sheffield clubbing to a different level. It would have been open now had the original application been granted as it should have been."

Neil Midgley remembers how hard the fight was to land it and the lengths they had to go to to prove their case. He said:

"Anwar made it his mission to take on the establishment and win the license. Anyone else would have admitted defeat but Anwar was extremely determined. He took on anyone that got in his way. There had been no new nightclub licenses granted in Sheffield for years prior to Republic, but our successful appeal changed the whole policy of the licensing committee.

"On appeal we had to prove there was a 'need' for a new license. One argument was that other venues in the city went over capacity regularly - I remember over a few weekends hiding near the entrances to Music Factory, Leadmill, Kiki's etc and clickering people going in to prove they went over capacity."

The venue offered daytime cafe, gallery and exhibition space, office accommodation and more.

It's initial door policy was: "dress up, dress down, dress middle, dress round, we want you for your heart and not for your Armani shirt".

It opened its doors in late 1995 to huge anticipation. The interior was truly staggering and blended the heavy industry of Steel City with 20th century clubbing chic.

The Republic incorporated many original design features, including the giant industrial crane that teetered above the dance floor.

It created a very underground feel

The opening of Bed

for a venue that had to attract a very large, mass market to balance the books.

It truly tried to do things differently. Admission prices and bar charges were kept affordable and attitude was far more important than dress style when it came to admission policy.

Sally Jordan was one of the first through the door. She said: "The Republic was breathtaking. It was like something out of a Terminator movie. We couldn't quite believe we'd got something that amazing in sunny Sheffield."

Sadly, it didn't last long under its original ownership and the administrators were called in within a few months of opening but, bizarrely, things seemed to move up a gear

after that and it really started to build into a formidable business with a clutch of very popular nights - both midweek and weekend.

House and garage were the mainstay of the weekend with 'superstar' DJs like Jeremy Healy and Roger Sanchez performing, whilst the likes of Disco 2000 indie night and the Bomb student night were keeping the tills ringing in the week.

Neil Midgley admits the lack of experience of the original Republic team was the problem. He said: "It was clear straight away that we didn't know what we were doing. None of us had enough experience to promote a venue of that size. Fundamental ingredients which make a good venue, especially sound and light system, were not adequate and the music policy was far too underground for a club with a 1400 capacity."

But it took its sale to Gatecrasher to turn the Republic into one of the most successful venues of the era as the Birmingham brand developed its quest for after dark domination.

The club night that had already had highly successful residencies at the Arches and the Adelphi in Sheffield decided it was time to settle down and have a place it could call home.

The Republic name was eventually resigned to history as it was revamped and renamed Gatecrasher One. Even a high profile drugs raid in early 2000 couldn't dent its popularity.

Every name DJ worth his or her salt spun the decks at the venue together with a worthy local resident, one Matt Hardwick.

Neil Midgley ended up returning to work at The Republic as part of the Gatecrasher team. He has fond memories.

"Going back to work for Gatecrasher at Republic was great. The Trance scene was exploding

and Gatecrasher was literally the global centre of it. Many times I'd go off to buy a sandwich at lunch-time and tourists would be lining up to have their photo taken next to the Lion logo on the side of the building. I remember the night the Chemical Brothers turned up as customers, months later they released 'Hey Boy, Hey Girl' said to be written about their experience at Gatecrasher.

"Demand was so high for the Saturday night between 1998 and 2000, staff seemed to spend most of the week taking phone calls trying to deter people coming if they hadn't got tickets. People were travelling from all over the UK. Coaches stretched the length of Matilda Street every week.

"I was employed to work on events Monday to Friday, while everyone else concentrated on the Gatecrasher night. The midweek nights (Disco 2000, Blessed, Bubblegum) soon became amazingly successful as well. I remember the decision to serve discount Vodka & Redbull (which was a new craze) seemed to kick start them all, and having a free rein

to develop them was really exciting.

"The owner Simon Raine along with his partners Simon Oates and Scott Bond were formidable.. Raine was a very driven business man, and Scott Bond was a big player in the Trance scene. They saw the importance of big name DJs at the time and were one step ahead in looking after them and signing exclusivity deals.

"I think their Millennium event at Don Valley Stadium was the peak of their success. Many events nationally didn't succeed that night, but Gatecrasher sold-out 40,000 tickets and could have probably sold 10,000 more."

Although the building will be best remembered as the permanent home of Gatecrasher (it burnt down a few years later), it also played host to ground-breaking gigs in its early Republic days.

Everyone from the Longpigs to Pulp graced the stage.

It was also one of the first venues to have an email address. You could drop a line to ben@republic.win. uk.net as long ago as 1996.

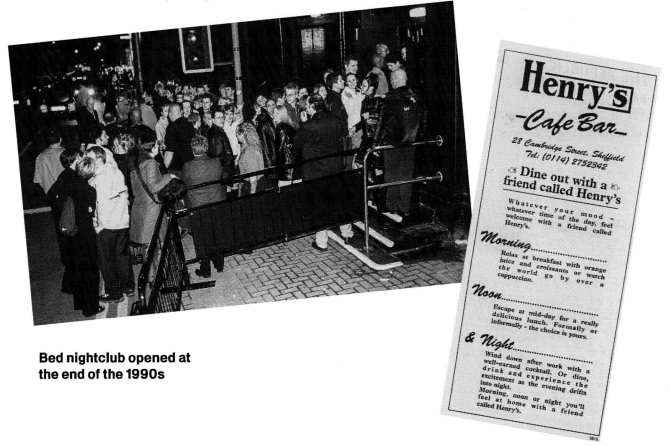

Bed nightclub opened at the end of the 1990s

Henry's
Cafe Bar

28 Cambridge Street, Sheffield
Tel: (0114) 2752342

Dine out with a friend called Henry's

Whatever your mood – whatever time of the day, feel welcome with a friend called Henry's.

Morning....
Relax at breakfast with orange juice and croissants or watch the world go by over a cappuccino.

Noon....
Escape at mid-day for a really delicious lunch. Formally or informally - the choice is yours.

& Night....
Wind down after work with a well-earned cocktail. Or dine, drink and experience the excitement as the evening drifts into night.
Morning, noon or night you'll feel at home with a friend called Henry's.

Andrea Jones said: "God, I had some of the best nights of my life at Republic. What an awesome venue!"

Phil Oakey at the Bed nightclub opening

The Music Factory in action

Neil Barlow of the Republic said: "I remember seeing the very stylish flyers produced by the Designers Republic and thinking that it was a venue I had to go and see. Inside was amazing, 3 floors with different music and Playstations set up on the balcony in the main room - ace memories."

☺The Jam Factory at the Locarno/Palais Nightclub

Laura Hayes remembers the beginnings of cutting edge dance nights:

"When four students hired the Locarno on London Road in the winter of 1988 it was the start of a new dynamic dance club that became known all over the north and for a time rivalled the neighbouring big name club The Hacienda in Manchester. Two girls and two boys, from four very different cultures met through University and a shared love of politics and club culture. Anantini Krishnan, a medical student from Thailand, lived with Laura Dove, an English student from London and they met up with DJ Anwar Akhtar from Manchester and Jerome Curran from Irish Catholic Northern Ireland's border country. Sheffield and Sheffield Hallam Universities formed the target market for a new one off party, that was held on a Wednesday. The first party was a big success, and this led to the formation of Mainstream Music Management which did a deal to run a regular slot called Compulsion on a Wednesday night. Compulsion quickly gained a reputation for cutting edge dance music, with DJ Anwar bringing on board his partner in crime DJ Simon 'Green' Mander. The club Locarno was an iconic building that looked very different but had hit hard times when the new team took over. The club's owner was formerly agent to Paul Young, and only known as Big George, he gave the student team full run of the club in early 1989 to put on a major new night on a Saturday. The ambition was to take on the Leadmill club and to keep the big student population partying in Sheffield at the weekends, rather than the mass exodus to Leeds, Nottingham and Manchester which had started to happen. Laura had attending some big warehouse parties in London Kings Cross including one run by indie band Primal Scream called the Jam Factory. The name was exported to Sheffield and with a name change to launch the night the Palais was born and the Sheffield Jam Factory kicked off with guest super star DJs imported from London, Manchester and Leeds. Anwar and Green continued to play the main slots with special guests to spice up the nights. The Palais attracted a big crowd for the next 3 years, and included a unique mix of Detroit sounds along side the unique sound of Sheffield which included the trade mark techno sound, epitomised by the Forgemasters. The club management eventually started a student Thursday indie night and a pure hardcore Friday night which featured big stars such as Carl Cox alongside local toasting DJs. The club was successful for these three years, before eventually the club began to wane in popularity, which was also being seen in other clubs around the country. Drugs were starting to become a major issue, and despite changing security teams, this culminated in a major riot in 1990 with the police invading the club and closing it down for some time. At that point the university students fell out and broke up the team, although Anwar and Jerome continued to work in the club into late 1992. The Palais is today now a Sainsbury's but is still a major iconic building in the city. It has a great past of providing brilliant tunes, inspiring music that reached across all divides. It was a great time in dance culture in Sheffield and will not be forgotten."

London Road's Palais is rocked to its foundation

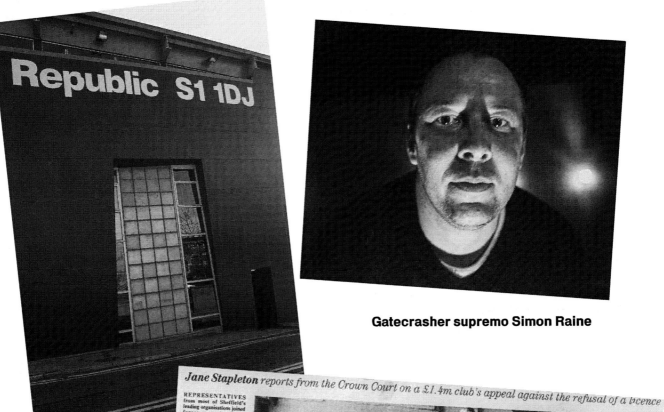

Gatecrasher supremo Simon Raine

The Republic

Jane Stapleton reports from the Crown Court on a £1.4m club's appeal against the refusal of a licence

REPRESENTATIVES from most of Sheffield's leading organisations joined forces yesterday in an attempt to persuade a Crown Court judge that the city needed a new night club to help revitalise its image and popularity.

Supporters crowded into the courtroom for the appeal which has been brought because licensing magistrates turned down the application for the £1.4m night spot, exhibition and conference centre in a disused factory building on the corner of Matilda Street and Arundel Street in the designated cultural industries quarter of the city.

The magistrates' original decision was based on the grounds that there was no need for another pub licence in the area. This is supported at the current hearing by opponents to the proposal, city night clubs, Kiki's, Isabella's and the Leadmill.

John Hughill QC, representing the club, said there was immense backing for the club which, it was felt, would play an integral role in the cultural industries quarter.

He said it was already a very successful area which had attracted 100 companies. "It is felt by a lot of people that these premises will form a vital part of the regeneration of of the city.

"The reason there are so many people here with so much to say about it is because there are so many interests involved."

He added: "The city itself backs this particular appeal because it is felt to be so important for the area.

Apart from the trade objectors everyone is in favour of it."

One of the first witnesses was the city's director of tourism, Dr John Heeley. He repeated his fears that, without regeneration, investment and ideas, the centre could be doomed.

He said there was a vibrant outer ring of attractions such as the Arena, Don Valley Stadium and Meadowhall. "There is a great need to anchor tourism much more firmly in the city centre otherwise there is a threat of the 'doughnut' effect resulting in a run-down or completely empty core."

Paul Skelton, of the city council's department of employment and economic development, said the cultural quarter had been earmarked to develop cultural industries when it was set up six years ago as a ten year project.

Levels of mainly private investment were already approaching £25m and 100 different businesses had set up in the area with the majority surviving despite the recession, proving that it was a stable and unique business centre.

However, added Mr Skelton, the quarter needed something like the proposed club to advertise its success and exploit its full potential.

"We have developed a production base second to none outside London in cultural industries. A night club would give support to the business community, would be used by the business community and also provide a showcase for the quarter."

He said the proposal was important because it was more than just a night club and it would provide varied facilities upwards of 16 hours a day.

It was also a watershed in terms of a wholly privately funded scheme on such a grand scale.

A report from planning consultant, Dr John Montgomery, revealed there was a definite need for a night club in the city centre.

Dr Montgomery said his data, based on a 30-minute drive time, showed the city centre was catching only 32% of the potentially available trade. The rest was going to clubs elsewhere such as Leeds, Manchester and Nottingham.

Sheffield Development Corporation chief executive Graham Kendall supported the appeal, saying outskirts developments such as Meadowhall and Bourbon Street, needed to be balanced and complemented by inner-city development.

"It is without doubt that Sheffield city centre has been in decline for several years. People are simply not going into the centre and there is a danger that the spiral of decline will increase. We believe this proposal will be an advantage and will make a contribution towards the overall regeneration of the area."

The case is expected to last for at least another day after today's business when it will be adjourned into the New Year.

● Bourbon Street all-clear:

Club appeal backed

The entrepreneurs behind the club project: Neil Midgley, Jerome Carran, Anwar Akhtar, Tony Fitzgerald and Fran Hilbert

The Republic Club/Bar/Art

Venue. The Old Roper & Wreaks Works. 112 Arundel Street. Sheffield S1 1DJ
Postal Address. Suite 10. Units 508-511. The Workstation. 15 Paternoster Row. Sheffield S1 2BX

Original visual for The Republic

THE EAST END TRIES TO GET IN ON THE AFTER DARK ACT

CHAPTER FOUR

A Star Readers' Club outing

Few areas were more representative of the speculative nature of 1990s nightlife in Sheffield than its East End.

Meadowhall had already proved how easy it was to stem the lifeblood of the city centre's retail experience. By the second half of the 1990s it would be Valley Centertainment's turn to try and inflict insurmountable damage to its evening economy.

The sprawling Sheffield Arena was one of the first after dark venues to establish itself in the area in the 1990s - it opened in May 1991 and reshaped the live music scene in the region.

Pulse/Vogue/Hotshots was the first club to open in the East End that offered serious competition to the city centre - they opened just a few hundred yards from the Arena.

It was a sprawling aircraft hangar of an after dark opportunity that cost Rank a cool £8million.

It was big, brash and shamelessly mainstream.

They got around the lack of nearby feeder bars by building their own - Hotshots. And they provided a free bus service from the city centre to get the punters down there.

There's no doubt the potential audience was within their grasp - they'd also got nearby Rotherham, Doncaster and Chesterfield to plunder if Sheffield wasn't delivering enough people to occupy their 1,875 capacity.

Rank threw everything at the venture; the cost of the free bar alone at the glitzy VIP launch would have been enough to buy a sizeable pad in upmarket Dore.

No expense spared lightshow, sound system and decor completed the gargantuan experience and nights on offer spanned everything from 'More Fun Than Your Mum' midweek student outing to commercial dance and chart at the weekend.

Hotshots was a aircraft hangar-style bar filled with video arcade games and more; Pulse was the nightclub aimed at the 18-25s whilst Vogue was targeting the older market.

It was very American and called itself an "entertainment complex".

The city centre held its breath... Was this going to be the first serious body blow to existing venues? It didn't have to wait very long. The multi-million pound experiment failed and it shut.

Though it was eventually sold, it wasn't reopened as a nightspot. Barnsley-based Brook Leisure transferred the license to their new venue in Barker's Pool, Kingdom (now known as Embrace).

Pulse/Vogue/Hotshots ended up as office space.

Jody Ball: "I was sad when Pulse and Vogue shut. I really did think it offered something different and the bus ride down there was one of the most raucous experiences of my life!"

The story wasn't much better at Valley Centertainment's massive Club Wow which opened in November 1998. Though it had more of an innings, these days it's a kids play centre.

At 2,300 capacity, it dwarfed anything in the city centre and was owned by First Leisure which also operated Brannigans which, at the time, was doing pretty brisk business downstairs.

Club Wow cost £5.5million. It was the icing on the cake for the Valley Centertainment complex that was now seriously taking shape with enormous multi-plex cinema and growing array of eateries.

The award for one of the fastest openings and closings in the area must be reserved for the Players Cafe.

The venue was opened by Def Leppard's Joe Elliot and Rick Savage together with Tim Cranson of Sheffield Steelers Ice Hockey Team.

It's unique offer was the fact it was going to be a magnet for all the local stars and if you fancied rubbing shoulders with any of them, you needed to make it your destination.

Sadly the Players, which was housed in the former Carbrook School, didn't last long enough for many people to put the theory into practice. The only time it seemed to get busy was as a pre-bar for the nearby Sheffield Arena.

The one thing it will be noted for was the fantastic party it hosted for the launch of The Full Monty DVD. Never have so many soap stars got so drunk under one roof in Sheffield - if the Players were picking up the tab it's no surprise they went under.

Wendy Marsh said: "I remember being sat in between Les Battersby and Jimmy Corkhill in one of the bars - they were both absolutely leathered."

Learning the art of a '90s haircut

☺It was never too late to party...

John Quinn said: "It is sometimes said that youth is wasted on the young. No it isn't. As someone who spent most of my teenage years and early 20s engrossed in the Sheffield scene, the 1990s represented more of the same but little that seemed brand new, to me at least.

"I can remember, on an early visit to the Leadmill, talking to someone who admitted being in her mid-20s and thinking: "Wow! Imagine still going clubbing at that advanced age. I'll definitely never be that sad." By the dawn of the 1990s I was that age. And I was that sad.

"However age, or something, has taken its toll, as although I have very vivid memories of my early '80s nights out (first pub The Hornblower, first 'club' Stars, first snog The Limit) the following decade is much less clearer in my head. Not that there was any snogging. I'd taken a vow of celibacy, or to be precise, the rest of the human race had decided upon it for me.

"But despite that there were some good nights, as the city's scene expanded, with new venues and new faces springing up all the time and even some of the older characters - well, slightly older than me - making it to national fame.

"Of course there still were events specifically designed for the... er...more mature customer. The '60s nights at the Leadmill were an example, where teenagers who had just discovered The Beatles mixed with those for whom the Fab Four were part of their teenage years. But it could be confusing. I was to find out that my own dad, who had no interest at all in pop music, had once - briefly - visited with a couple of mates who he'd had a few with and were all under the impression that it was an over-60s night...

"The closure of the legend that was The Limit in the early '90s left a void in the city's nightlife. A dark, stinking, sticky and overflowing with urine void (and that was before you even reached the toilets) but a void nonetheless. Although this hole was never properly filled during the '90s, most of the clientele simply transferred to other venues. For those of a rock leaning there was always Rebels, although it would probably take less time to climb the Rock Of Gibraltar than those endless flights of stairs. It was much easier to get into The Corporation which is probably why it is still thriving to this day.

"The Leadmill meanwhile was still the best bet for those of a vaguely indie leaning, with regular concerts and discos covering various styles from Madchester - although of course the really ahead of the times would have seen Happy Mondays support The Shamen of all people there in 1987 - to Britpop - during the glory days of which I witnessed Justine from Elastica kick Pulp's Russell up the arse as he walked past. Nice to see our local heroes get treated with such respect. The dancier types meanwhile headed for Occasions, where Warp's records ruled the roost.

"As well as these permanent places, some venues best known for other stuff held modern music-orientated events. Drop played some great music (and admittedly some awful stuff too) if you could cope with the unedifying sight of grown men wearing shorts - something that is only vaguely tolerable in the gym or on the beach but not in the hallowed surroundings of the City Hall Ballroom. Whatever happened to dignity and standards? I'd have loved to see some waltzing in tuxedos and long dresses to the relaxing sounds of Rage Against The Machine.

"Some people did turn up in suits to Brighton Beach in the middle of the decade, which launched as part of the Britpop-inspired mod revival (or whatever it was) and that venue was also the scene of regular '70s nights, which again played some superb sounds - albeit often so cheesy you could have put them in a sandwich - and those who made the effort to get dressed up in suitable garb showed a considerable amount of (wait for it) flair. Geddit? It's a pun on 'flare.' As in flared trousers.

"As for the dance scene and all the myriad permutations, I was no expert . One place I did visit several times was what was Tiffanys on London Road. During the '90s it seemed to change its name every week. The Palais. Bed. Music Factory. And now Sainsbury's. The music's gone downhill but on the other hand you rarely need to queue to get in and they're unlikely to run out of booze.

"Possibly the biggest dance music success of that decade was Gatecrasher, which started off in the Midlands before establishing a base in Sheffield, most notably at the dearly-departed Republic According to the fountain of all knowledge that is Wikipedia, the door policy was 'notoriously strict.' It couldn't have been that strict though as someone as averse as I to dressing up even on special occasions (or even for Occasions) got in with no problem at all on my three or so attempts. Could never quite work out what that babies' dummies bit was about. Probably something about looking back to lost childhoods. Talking of which, for some of us it, was lost a very long time ago. I need a nap."

Gatecrasher in '96 at the Adelphi

Gatecrasher in '96 at the Adelphi

East 17 meet fans

Sheffield star Dave Berry's popularity continued throughout the 1990s

life after dark

Vogue Nightclub

VOGUE: is an exclusive venue for clubbers who are over 25

VOGUE: Customers have free access to and from PULSE all night

VOGUE: is a mix of current chart music that you know and classics you've enjoyed

VOGUE: is a purpose built fully air conditioned nightclub that features state of the art sound and lighting along with excellent facilities for your comfort, enjoyment and security

25+

pulse

18+

PULSE, a programme of the best Dj's and PA's in the country, hosted by residents presenting a mix of dance music you know, anthems you've enjoyed and new tracks you'll grow to love

PULSE, a £5 million purpose built dance arena featuring state of the art sound, a breath taking laser and stunning lighting effects

PULSE, for people who enjoy clubbing to enjoy themselves, no pretensions, and no attitudes

OPEN: 10.00pm – Late Thursday to Saturday

DRESS: Smart casual (Thursday smart jeans O.K.)

AGE: Strictly over 18.

happylife

deep end

MONDAY **Totally Talent** Karaoke Night

TUESDAY **CAN U JAM?**

WEDNESDAY Room Hire Available

THURSDAY **LIVE MUSIC**

FRIDAY **Anything Goes**

SATURDAY **60's, 70's & 80's**

SUNDAY **ACID**

3 Bars on 2 Levels
POOL • BIG SCREEN • WAITING SERVICE
Not everything in Hillsborough Makes sense!

The Deep End
Former Hillsborough Baths, Langsett Road,
Hillsborough, Sheffield S6 2EN
Tel. 0114 285 4000

Dan Brookman who opened the popular Deep End in Hillsborough

TOP OF THE POPS

The Longpigs at Music In The Sun

CHAPTER FIVE

The one thing the city did maintain throughout the duration of the 1990s was its ability to produce hit makers.

Sheffield's rock'n'roll CV was regularly in demand in the era but not always for the right reason... It was under the scrutiny of the national media as they sought answers as to why the National Centre for Popular Music was taking root in Steel City and not their beloved London.

1997 publication, the 'Rock & Roll Traveller to Great Britain & Ireland', was one of many that fought our corner and reminded detractors we were more than worthy of taking the music crown north of Watford.

It said: "Outside the capital, England's fifth largest city, has consistently produced more quality rock acts since the '60s than any other metropolis, bar Manchester."

The 1990s truly belonged to Jarvis Cocker and Pulp - the band and front man were a true soundtrack to many growing up in the era and a key part of the Britpop movement..

Though it took them nearly 15 years to make it big, success was massive and it stayed with them.

Pulp first formed in 1978 and went through a myriad of line-up changes and achieved a modicum of independent success.

But it was the release of 'His 'n' Hers' in 1994 and its follow up, 'Different Class', in 1995 that put them in a different league.

The latter album hit the number one spot and spawned four top ten singles - both 'Common People' and 'Sorted For E's & Wizz' both reached number two.

Their disco-influenced pop/rock coupled with Jarvis Cocker's "kitchen sink drama"-style lyrics truly struck a chord with the 1990s generation.

He went from gangly outsider of the eighties to sex symbol par excellence of the 1990s. Though Pulp was conveniently lumped in with the Britpop movement of the era, many would rightly argue they offered far more.

The band courted their fair share of controversy at their peak.

Jarvis Cocker gained blanket coverage thanks to a legendary hijinks at the 1996 BRIT Awards, where he invaded the stage in protest during pop singer Michael Jackson's performance of "Earth Song" and "wiggled his backside" at the audience.

After complaints by Jackson and his entourage, Jarvis

Cocker spent the night in Kensington Police Station charged with actual bodily harm and assaulting the child performers.

Though he was later released without charge, the incident undoubtedly propelled Jarvis Cocker into areas no Pulp performance ever could have achieved. Record sales soared as a result.

The record company couldn't have wished for better publicity than the release of the band's 'Sorted For E's & Wizz' resulted in. Paranoia about the effects of ecstasy (or 'E' as it was better known) was at its height.

The Daily Mirror got things off to a flying start by printing a full page story that said 'BAN THIS SICK STUNT' alongside a story that said the song was "pro-drugs".

The record company marketing department must have been working overtime (or whoever it was that came up with the idea) as the single also had an inlay which showed how to conceal amphetamines in a DIY 'wrap'

Jarvis Cocker released a statement saying: "...'Sorted' is not a pro-drugs song. Nowhere on the sleeve does it say you are supposed to put drugs in here but I understand the confusion. I don't think anyone who listens to 'Sorted' would come away thinking it had a pro-drugs message."

The 'confusion' helped the single come dangerously close to being top of the charts and 'sorted' ended up becoming part of the English language.

The city's Longpigs kept their career far more succinct. They had both their rise and fall in the era.

The alternative rock act enjoyed success at the fringe of the Britpop explosion. Their 1996 debut album, 'The Sun Is Often Out', was deservedly voted one of the year's best albums by both Q and Melody Maker. Singles like 'She Said' and 'On and On' were regularly bothering the singles charts.

The band comprised vocalist Crispin Hunt, guitarist Richard Hawley, bassist Simon Stafford and drummer Dee Boyle.

They were lined up for greatness. They were starting to be well received in America and even opened for U2 on several dates of their gargantuan global Popmart Tour.

They lost the momentum with the release of second album 'Mobile Home'; their record company folded and the Longpigs went the same way not long after.

All in all, it was an incredibly productive time for music. Blameless were flown to the States to record. Olive seemed to come from nowhere

and score a number one with 'You're Not Alone'.

Speedy narrowly missed a hit with 'Boy Wonder'. Babybird got in everyone's head with 'You're Gorgeous' and Moloko hit the big time towards the end of the era with 'Sing It Back'.

Etiquette hit the national headlines for taking rapper/actor Ice T and his band Bodycount on a tour of Sheffield's more unsavoury nightspots.

So many great bands nearly (or should) have hit the big time; FINE, Lazy Dollies, Oblong, Bitter Lemon, the Astrids, the list goes on and on.

And whilst the younger upstarts were chomping at the bit there was plenty of activity from their elders.

The city organised 'Def Leppard Day' and gave the multi-million selling rock act plaques to unveil and tea with the mayor. The climax of the event was an invite only acoustic set at Sheffield rock bar the Wapentake.

Not to be outdone, Joe Cocker had a tree to plant and an honorary doctorate courtesy of Sheffield Hallam University.

Human League enjoyed a return to the charts and even turned on the city's Christmas Lights towards the end of the 1990s.

Austin Grant of Music In The Sun

☺David Dunn

"Landing fresh-faced and clean-livered, the '90s in Sheffield was a time of opportunity.

"The local band scene was really healthy, not least as it was a time that local favourites Pulp were beginning to break through to the wider world.

"While my brain is pretty hazy with regards a lot of gigs one of my favourites was Jarvis Cocker's lot at The Leadmill at Radio 1's Sound City event in '91 I think it was.

"They were on the cusp of greatness and after the gig Jarv stayed around on the dance floor. It was the highlight to a week during which there were sold out gigs every night at the Leady and the old Nelson Mandela Building at Hallam Uni. We used to dash between the venues when one band finished and another started.

"We managed to do the whole thing in the early hours all week and by the end of it - 6am kick-out on Sunday morning, my hearing and my voice were shot.

"As The Star's newly appointed music editor I lived to fight another day, fired up by the prospect of going to an endless flood of free gigs for as long as my shell-likes held out.

"Another truly memorable brace of gigs happened at what was The Hallamshire on West St.

"On one occasion a Japanese band called The Privates came to play, ahead of a weekend spot at Mexborough's Corner Pocket. They were like as big as U2 in their homeland but they played upstairs in this pub and brought enough gear to play City Hall.

"Japanese students came to see them as they posed around the pub beforehand and when they came on it was all foot on the monitor, crotch-grabbing rock. The first song was like that scene from 'Back To The Future' when Michael J Fox hits his guitar in front of the giant amp and is thrown against the wall. The sound here actually hurt and you could feel your chest being stoved in.

"Another classic at the same venue was a Scarborough band called Grandads Don't Indicate. They'd been in an accident not long before the gig and I think three of them turned up in bandages and plaster. Music was so so but the sight of them was hilarious.

"Another night Coventry band Adorable played up there and if memory serves me right it ended in the singer and guitarist hitting each other as the set climaxed on the rabble-rouser Homeboy.

"It was a sad day when the Hallamshire stopped hosting gigs, but succumbed to a refit after a fairly bruising final night during Pyjama Jump. Now that was a sight for sore thighs.

"Babybird at The Leadmill the week 'You're Gorgeous' went to number three in the charts sticks in the memory, not least when singer Stephen Jones lost his rag with a woman who was talking at the front of the crowd during the quiet tunes the crowd didn't really know.

"He stopped performing in order to tell her 'you're ruining my evening, you c***'. I guess it was the start of him hating that single as it was the only thing people had come for that evening. On the band's last show in Sheffield it didn't figure in their set.

"I did a very warts and all review colour piece next day which even the subs asked whether I really wanted to put through. It went in and Jones actually kind of thanked me later on for being frank and making him realise he had to adapt to difficult audiences. A volatile genius if ever there was one.

"I could probably recall some more under hypnosis but for now they've slipped under the clouds of time and too many late nights."

The Astrids

The Leadmill was landing landmark gigs left, right and centre in the era - Mel C's live performance attracted her fellow Spice Girls and one David Beckham

The Longpigs

Etiquette packed the Roundhouse for their single launch before imploding

Def Leppard visit Don Valley Stadium for 'Def Leppard Day'

Pulp - one of the city's biggest music exports of the era

THE RED CARPET TREATMENT

CHAPTER SIX

The Full Monty cast

The success of 'The Full Monty' truly caught Sheffield off guard. In fact it caught everyone associated with it off guard - cast and crew included.

Take Jim and Marie-Luise Coulthard who were happy to accept £400 for the use of a few minutes of footage from the long-forgotten Sheffield film they made in 1971, 'City On The Move'.

Originally filmed over two years, it portrayed the city at its most confident and formed the main thrust of a massive PR drive by the Town Hall.

Their footage, which fronts The Full Monty and was originally funded by the council, ended up as one of the flick's defining moments.

The Full Monty went on to become one of the highest grossing films in the history of cinema. If the Coulthards had been on a percentage of the film's earnings they could have probably bought the Town Hall with their loose change. Sadly they weren't...

The Coulthards took things in good grace as The Full Monty, a low budget comedy about six unemployed men - four of them ex steelworkers - forming a striptease outfit to raise much-needed cash, became an unexpected hit right around the globe.

Despite being light hearted, the movie addressed some pretty serious issues - unemployment, fathers' rights, depression, impotence,

homosexuality, obesity, working class culture and suicide.

For that reason it was hard not to feel empathy for the various down-at-heel characters.

Sadly, empathy for the film, or its characters, didn't stretch to some corners of the Town Hall.

The bigger the film got, the louder the mutterings got in the corridors of power in Sheffield that the film did not put Steel City in a good light and they should distance themselves from it.

It's fair to say the city wasn't used to being in this kind of intense, media spotlight.

Years on and you'll still find its detractors but most people are happy that it amply displayed the tenacity, warmth and humour of your average city dweller, even if they are on their

uppers.

Thankfully the male craze for striptease in the city, ignited by the film, has largely died down these days...

The Full Monty wasn't Sheffield's only dalliance on the silver screen in the era - far from it.

'Tales From A Hard City' was far nearer the knuckle as far as portrayal of Sheffield's underbelly was concerned.

The drama/documentary came out two years prior the Full Monty in 1995.

'Tales From A Hard City' majored on the lives of four unsavoury chancers from Sheffield.

It was described as 'a compelling documentary about four dreamers: the dirty dancer, the hustler, the thief and the media mogul, all looking for a break in Old Steel City'.

It became an award-winning cult classic.

Alex Usbourne, producer of the film, said: "Tales from a Hard City was about a moment in time. It was about looking at the Lower Don Valley and realising the steelworks had gone and then hearing the voices saying it's OK, we don't need industry we have shopping, leisure and sport.

"It was a film about Sheffielders adapting to this new age with a combination of blind panic and singular tenacity.

"It was also a film influenced and inspired by the amazing and original work of Dr. Geoffrey Beattie who was a psychologist at Sheffield University. "He seemed to spend all his time at Josephines nightclub and then write about it for The Guardian and in his seminal book 'Survivors of Steel City.' He showed us all that the best stories are right under your nose if only you look carefully enough and ask the right questions."

'When Saturday Comes' was another Sheffield offering of the era.

The local press was alive with its progress at the time. It starred Sean Bean as hard drinking footballer Jimmy Muir, with a supporting cast which included Pete Postlewhaite and real life Steel City soccer heroes, Tony Currie and Mel Sterland.

It got its premiere at Meadowhall followed by a show by local act, Big Wide World.

Even Prince Charles fell for the charms of The Full Monty

☺Mark Sheridan

"I was setting up one night and one of the regulars was sitting at the bar. In his mid twenties he was a member of the BBC and I don't mean the television company. It was my job to unhook the lights above the pool table and then move the pool table into the corner so that I could set up and the dance floor would be clear.

"Anyway, the guy called over to me "Are you still going to be playing shit music all night then like usual?"

"I replied "Well if you keep treating my equipment like a bouncy castle what do you expect?" "As soon as I had said this I immediately regretted it. I had seen this lad deck people just because he didn't like the look of them. I turned to him and saw he was sat still on his stool. "He just looked at me, laughed and said, "Y'know? You're alright mate".

"I never had any trouble from the BBC in that pub. Funny though because nearly every other DJ did!"

The only way was up in '90s Sheffield

Chris Porter said: "Though we never had our own Eastenders or Coronation Street, it's fair to say we had our share of success on the silver screen in the 1990s. They might not have been to everyone's liking but they certainly put the city on the map."

Crowds were out in force to see the 1971 film 'City On The Move' which got a new lease of life after part of it fronted The Full Monty

Even 'Blakey' got in on the clubbing act - he visited the city to help launch a new late night bus service

Gritty docu-drama Tales From A Hard City

**Creative entrepreneur
Simon Evans**

Leadmill staff get to grips with an early website

The joy of clubbing in the East End

CLUBLAND'S PROMOTIONAL BLIGHT

CHAPTER SEVEN

The council's Grimebusters squad declared war on graffiti and flyposting

Today's generation would probably look at you gone out as you mixed your wallpaper paste and set off down town with a brush and rolled up set of posters.

But in the 1990s, flyposting, for many, was seen as the only way to promote club nights and gigs.

Forget your Facebook wall or Twitter feed, we were still adapting to mobile phones being smaller than the housebrick-style ones of a few years earlier.

Whilst some saw flyposting as an art form, the Town Hall saw it as nothing but a blight on the city's landscape.

Things seriously came to head in 1994 when the Tidy Britain Group voted Sheffield as the country's 'Graffiti Capital'.

The media were awash with stories about the state of the city accompanied by visuals of graffiti and yes, flyposting.

The council fought back and launched its 'Grimebusters' service to start to remove graffiti and flyposting.

But as one poster was taken down, another was immediately stuck up. It became a cat and mouse game between the council and the venue promoters.

Sheffield's most prolific graffiti

artist was 'Fista', real name Simon Sunderland. He was the bane of the life of Liberal Democrat Councillor Francis Butler. He said at the time:

"I don't mind admitting it - he had me beat. I publicly acknowledged it: I was on the point of giving up.

"No one living outside of Sheffield can imagine the chaos he caused over the years. He painted on everything: walls, private houses, public buildings, street signs, even a bus that had broken down. The trouble was that as soon as we cleared it off, more would appear. We just didn't have the resources,

neither human nor financial, to cope.
It was an epidemic."

But even he was shocked at the
length of sentence handed down to
Fista in 1996 when he was eventually
caught. 23-year-old Simon
Sunderland was sent down for five
years.

The jail term was eventually
reduced to a year.

The flyposting wars carried on for
months until an agreement, of sorts,
was reached. It wasn't exactly rocket
science; a set of legal flyposting sites
were set up around the city. They're
still very much in use today.

**Grimebusters head Chris Spafford is on hand to help
councillors Jan Wilson and Jean Cromer**

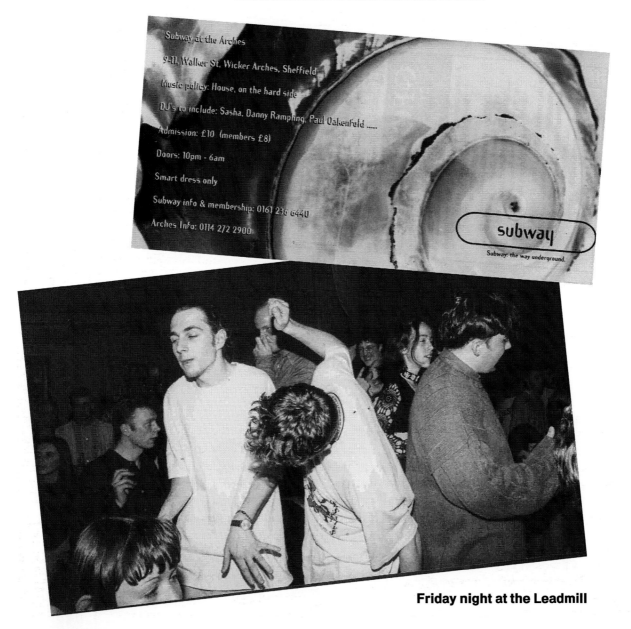

Friday night at the Leadmill

☺Taking dance back underground

The arrival of Headcharge in the late 1990s proved that innovation was still alive and kicking in the small hours of Sheffield.

The club could best be described as a post-apocalyptic clubbing experience. This was no place for your Day-Glo 'Crasher kids and no place for the faint hearted.

From day one it became a melting pot for all styles, ages and walks of life. Where clubbers mixed with old punks and hippies and all go generally mad to the sounds of techno, trance, nu-nrg, global breaks, beats, dub, d&b and more, on a strobe lit dance floor comprising Day-Glo paint, tattoos, piercings and happy faces.

Jamie Headcharge put it down to the city's love of danger.

"Why do we think that Headcharge has endured while so many clubs become flash-in-the-pans - huge one minute and gone the next? The world of clubland is a fickle one but Headcharge has always been very lucky with its crowd, who we believe to be one of the best in the country. Sheffield has a high percentage of party-head climbers who have always been a strong part of the Sheffield underground scene - there must be something that links their desire to risk their lives climbing vertical overhangs with a desire to dance all night in a sweaty club to fearsome techno music."

Headchargers had been known to turn up from as far away as Australia and Ibiza in the past!

Headcharge in action

Wapentake landlord Bob Mirfin
was only happy to meet one diehard Def Leppard who travelled
all the way from Japan to sample
the delights of the bar that
played host to the band in their
early days

Metal club night Reservoir Rocks was
a regular visitor to Hallam University's
Nelson Mandela building

Councillor Peter Price held his 60th birthday party in
the Rhythm Room flanked by council leader Mike Bower

beluga

24, Carver Street
Sheffield
S1 4FS
tel 0114 273 8677

West St
Division St
Carver St

Monday
Float and *Funk*
Global Acid Jazz and decadent latino funk
PILS £1.00 HAPPY HOUR ALL NIGHT

TUESDAY — WATCH OUT FOR

WEDNESDAY — UPBEAT AND COOL

THURSDAY — NIGHTS TO COME

Friday *FLOW*
MIDDLE OF THE ROAD
CHART AND DANCE

Saturday *SUBMERGED*
MIDDLE OF THE ROAD
CHART AND DANCE
LADIES FREE ENTRY ALL NIGHT
PILS £1.00 B4 10.30

UpYerRonson
PRESENTS
STEEL

Love to be...
...TUNED IN

Le Citrus
One of the most intriguing nights of the era arrived just shy of the Millennium. It was Le Citrus at the Casbah.
Never has so many slices of fresh lemon and orange hung from the ceiling of a single venue.
The midweek event was a true enigma and was packed from the day it opened its doors.

Naseem Hamed enjoyed near world domination in the era

Human League in the 1990s

Reclaim the streets protest

Bob Worm remembers the early days of the Arches:

"The venue opened in 1994 with the first legal all night entertainment license in Sheffield after me and several other people spent a week out on the city centre streets with clipboards getting signatures to support the license being granted.

"The venue wasn't allowed to sell alcohol at this point and the first nights promoted were Happy Hardcore nights by the legendary Edge Club team from Coventry.

"These went well for a while and then the club soon discovered its main problem; running one or two nights on a Friday and Saturday was not bringing in enough money to make ends meet.

"The club then put out its own house night called Subway with the likes of DJ Sasha, then a top star on the scene. The first night on a very hot mid summer evening was packed to the walls.

"Needless to say the event was a huge success and started what was a regular night of top quality house DJ's monthly.

"Then along came Gatecrasher for a Bank Holiday special, which packed the club. The night became a regular resident night for many months. This is where the Sheffield Gatecrasher legend was born and grew before it moved first to the Adelphi and Leadmill for one off's, before its bigger bank holiday specials at the Republic brought about the Gatecrasher team buying the Republic and the rest is history.

"The Arches in the meantime went through many ups and downs and along the way many promoters came and went. This seemed to be a bigger focus on Friday nights, with a mixture of house and techno or trance style events. This was all kick started by Smokescreen hosting a free party there which opened the doors to the free party crew Curfew hosting their Lifemind nights at the club. In 1996, the Return To The Source team came along, before Sheffield promoters called No Logic and a team from Manchester, who did techno nights had a regular successful run of doing Friday nights for a year."

ALL NIGHT CLUBBING WASN'T ON THE 24 HOUR CITY AGENDA

One of the most baffling competitions of the 1990s was that fought between different towns and cities eager to hail themselves as a '24 hour city'.

Sheffield seemed intent on putting itself forward as forerunner for the title but, at that point, to the layperson at least, we seemed to have little more to offer than a 24 hour Spar on Ecclesall Road and a couple of round-the-clock garages.

It's fair to say the '24 hour city' concept was badly marketed and fraught with potential PR problems.

The confusion was more than borne out with many people, unsurprisingly, ending up associating the concept as an argument for more bars, more nightclubs, all night drinking and, as a result, round the clock carnage.

News reports about the apparent virtues of a '24 hour city' were regularly accompanied by a picture of someone lying inebriated in the gutter. The true concept, which was about anything other than alcohol abuse, was normally lost in the accompanying brouhaha.

Anyone that attended the 24 Hour City Conference, hosted by Sheffield, in 1996 would have heard more of the true story.

The Crucible Theatre event was attended by city centre managers, town planners, architects and academics from around the country and Europe, in some cases.

They were debating how to improve towns and cities at night and reduce crime. One of the main things they argued for was encouraging people to move back, to living in town and city centre areas to cut down crime.

But they also proved, which thankfully wasn't reported at the time, they could also do their bit for all-night partying.

The delegate tour of the city's bars and clubs which happened on the opening night of the event went on that late it succeeded in ensuring half the attendees missed their alarm

calls and didn't attend their first session of the second day until the following afternoon!

The one venue that they didn't visit (it was a Thursday night and it didn't open) was Sheffield's true all-night venue, Niche.

It was Niche by name, Niche by nature. The Sidney Street operation ran from 12 midnight to 12 noon every Saturday and Sunday morning.

It was the sister club of Capitol, the dance club situated on Matilda Street that ran for a period in the 1990s.

It wasn't that long after the 1996 conference that many things argued for in the '24 hour city' concept actually started to happen

Sprawling complexes like West One began to appear on the city's skyline and thousands of people now live back in the city centre.

Ecstasy death changes the clubbing landscape

The death of schoolgirl Leah Betts in November 1995 brought the subject of Ecstasy to people's attention like never before.

She'd taken the drug on her 18th birthday and was in a coma four hours later.

Though her parents had allowed her to celebrate at home, they'd purposely stayed in to ensure there was no chance of illegal drugs being present.

Leah Betts never regained consciousness, she died a few days later.

Her parents became high profile anti-drugs campaigners.

Nobody could ignore what was going on under their noses anymore.

Illegal drugs were intrinsically linked to the dance scene.

Josephine's, which originally opened in the mid-1970s, got totally disillusioned with the direction of the after dark scene. It's owner, Dave Allen, ended up pulling the plug at the end of the era.

Nimmo's venue on Sidney Street

Josephines owner Dave Allen

The cross-dressing carnage of the Pyjama Jump - an event now consigned to history

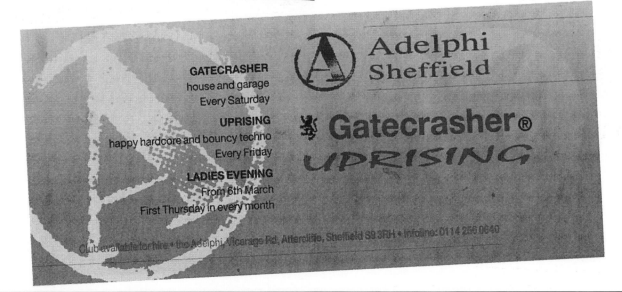

Clubbing in '96

Clubbing in '96

DROP VERSUS THE BALLROOM DANCERS

CHAPTER NINE

'Drop' regulars

The 1990s were regularly a troubled time for the rock scene in the city. Sheffield lost its legendary Rebels venue - the club that existed seven flights up on Dixon Lane.

The rise of grunge knocked the hair metal scene, that dominated the late 1980s, sideways.

Grandmasters of metal like the city's own Bruce Dickinson of Iron Maiden and Joe Elliot of Def Leppard were two of the first to visit the hairdressers.

It was Sheffield promoters Steve Stevlor and Mark 'Mutley' Hobson who truly captured the mood with their crossover night, Drop.

Running in the City Hall's Ballroom, the event blended rock, indie and alternative. It's fair to say anyone slightly leftfield found a home there.

But the arrival of hundreds of pairs of Para boots and Dr Martens didn't go down well with the blue-rinse daytime set who'd been tripping the light fantastic on the maple sprung dance floor since the 1930s.

They were not at all happy about sharing their much loved venue with the hundreds that attended faithfully on a Friday night.

They accused Drop audiences of wrecking the floor. The arguments were played out very publically in the media.

At one point the ballroom dancers thought they'd won the day and the floor was covered with rubber to protect it.

But Steve Stevlor said things didn't quite go according to plan: "Health and Safety reported it as a trip hazard and it was all ripped up again!"

He successfully argued that City Hall was only being used for the purpose it was built for.

"I was interviewed on BBC Radio Sheffield at the time and said; 'The City Hall was built for the young people of Sheffield to dance in and that exactly what's happening now'."

Ironically, these days, Steve Stevlor actually spends his Friday nights not listening to loud punk rock but ballroom dancing!

He said: "I took it up a few years ago and have been loving it ever since. I have lessons every Friday night!"

Mark Hobson ended up opening his own rock club in late 1997 to fill the hole left by the closure of Rebels. It was an ambitious move.

The scene was on its uppers and he took on the former Cairos, one of the largest venues in the city.

But the venue proved very popular and Drop found a new home.

DIRTY STOP OUTS .COM

'Drop' at City Hall Ballroom

The popular Wapentake bar

Corporation on Bank Street

A blessing disguise - the opening of Corporation

'Hotpants' DJ, the Dean of Disco

'Drop' regulars

The omni-present Johnny Loco

CITY COMES UNSTUCK WITH ITS MUSIC VISITOR ATTRACTION

CHAPTER TEN

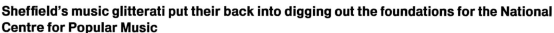

Sheffield's music glitterati put their back into digging out the foundations for the National Centre for Popular Music

Few things were as eagerly awaited in Sheffield as the £15m National Centre for Popular Music.

Nobody could quite believe the Lottery-funded project was going to be built in the city. Londoners were gobsmacked but, as they were reminded at the time, we thought of the idea first.

The National Centre for Popular Music should have been the city's visitor attraction numero Uno and then some. Recriminations as to the reason it failed were pored over for years.

Fact is, the public voted with their feet and the estimate of 400,000 visitors per year - the figure the entire business plan was built on - were widely off the mark.

The stainless steel, futuristic drum-shaped structure caused many a double-take as it took its place on the Steel City skyline but it was all accepted with good grace - music was regularly controversial, it wasn't surprising that a nod to such an art form would carry on in the same vein.

Many people were convinced NCPM was going to be the UK's answer to the Rock And Roll Hall of Fame in Ohio - the memorabilia-filled attraction that turned round the fortunes of another place that was built on steel, Cleveland.

There wasn't, it has to be said, much else worldwide to use as a benchmark - it was in largely unchartered territory.

Thoughts of failure never entered anyone's head.

Everyone loved music - what could go wrong?

For years the NCPM had been the focus of Tim Strickland, former Specials front man prior to the arrival of Terry Hall, and the venue's creative director.

Music memorabilia ended up being the last thing on the mind of the NCPM. The finished product surprised everyone, and sadly, not always in a good way.

The building was meant to be start of a new dawn for Sheffield's burgeoning Cultural Industries Quarter - the area set aside by the council for new and creative businesses which already contained after dark landmarks like The Leadmill and The Republic.

NCPM was going to provide much needed daytime footfall and new businesses were already opening up in readiness.

The dark clouds were already circling at the press launch. There was a struggle to get big name celebrities to the opening. The one that did turn up, Frank Skinner, went on the record to liken the place to "a giant Fisher Price toy".

It was all downhill from there. The noise from the public and press alike were that they were decidedly underwhelmed and visitors numbers were very poor.

NCPM was soon being cited in the same breath as the Dome in London which was another Lottery-funded project that was performing badly, and the failing Earth Centre in Doncaster.

It was facing the very real prospect of closure within weeks of opening and it was under siege from the media.

It was a sad state of affairs. Getting a job there had been a dream come true for so many, it had now turned into a total nightmare.

NCPM's last hope was to persuade its creditors (and there were many) to vote in favour of a CVA (company voluntary arrangement) - this meant they would write off a lot of what they were owed and give a lifeline to the project.

Sheffield's music legacy became the focus for its 'Teenage Kicks' exhibition and the positive reaction helped persuade creditors voting in favour of giving it new lease of life.

Sadly, new centre director Martin King managed to hammer one of the final nails in the coffin when the press got wind he'd landed a new job in London, without tellling anyone in Sheffield.

The venue soldiered on a while longer with some pretty impressive club nights but even that wasn't enough to save it from becoming Sheffield Hallam Students Union.

Thankfully the NCPM debacle was small at the side of the World Student Games but it was still a true body blow to the confidence of the city's music scene. It took the success of the Arctic Monkeys to start to restore it.

David Dunn said: "Bizarrely, it was Rotherham's Magna Centre that many people were writing off before it opened. Doncaster's Earth Centre was floundering, many thought Magna would follow - most people thought the National Centre for Popular Music was a done deal of success."

☺Independent promoters were the lifeblood of the scene

Sheffield was rife with the rise and fall of club nights.

Two of its most successful were undoubtedly NY Sushi and Viva Salsa. Both nights left an indelible mark on the after dark scene of the era.

At its height, NY Sushi were bringing hundreds to its events at Sheffield Ski Village, the venue had seen nothing like it.

Viva Salsa brought top Latin American artists and vibes to the city like never before and led to the opening of Cubana, the popular bar and restaurant that still thrives on Trippet Lane today.

**The 1996 Dirty Stop Outs
tour of Sheffield venues**

NEW YEAR'S EVE

Former council chief executive Bob Kerslake and his wife (middle) weren't strangers to the city's nightscene

The absolute zenith of the clubbing calendar in the 1990s was New Year's Eve and it didn't come much better than 1995, as Sheffield was becoming renowned as a true party capital.

Promoters responded accordingly by hiking up the admission price to otherwise outrageous levels. But in many respects they'd got little choice if they wanted to get the big DJ names that would pack the punters in.

As The Star said of New Year's Eve 1995 at the time: "Promoters are promising the most spectacular night of the year and have spent more than £50,000 to attract the best DJs."

Tickets ranged from £36 to get in the Arches to £7 for Niche.

One of the most expensive events to stage was the Music Factory's 'Love to be...' which was costing £30,000.

But it didn't deter the punters, far from it. The London Road club had virtually sold out of its 1,380 tickets, to see leading DJ Roger Sanchez and others mixing the tunes, days before.

Love to be... promoter Tony Gedge said of the event: "Sanchez is one of the most renowned re-mixers in the world and has worked with the best, including Michael Jackson. We are also flying down some bagpipe players from Scotland to bring in the New Year. It's all to celebrate an excellent year and start '96 in style."

The Arches offered leading British DJ Sasha whilst the Republic featured an all star line up including Dave Camacho and Harvey.

Trash at Kikis, on Charter Square, renowned for its outrageous costumes and cross-dressing, featured Princess Julia and Rachel Auburn with £20 tickets for non-members.

There really was little let up for the bank balances of the dance generation.

But we were still amateurs at the side of Manchester. Their Hacienda was charging £50 a head the same year.

Boxing Day was also a big date on the calendar with big admission prices to match.

These days nightclubs are lucky if they have two busy

nights a week.

Things were far more buoyant in the mid-1990s.

No role was more aspirational than that of being a club promoter.

Weekdays were alive with new club nights. There was always something being tried.

Retro mod night 'Brighton Beach' came to town, it still happens today.

Even Lord Mayors were getting in on the act.

The city's 100th first citizen, Councillor Peter Price, cut short the traditional Town Hall farewell reception to take colleagues clubbing.

He hired the nearby Rhythm Room to dance the night away whilst reminiscing about his year in office.

The outgoing chap was already no stranger to nineties clubbing. His inauguration saw him don crepes and drapes for his own rock'n'roll gig and he donned flares to officially open the Roundhouse nightclub.

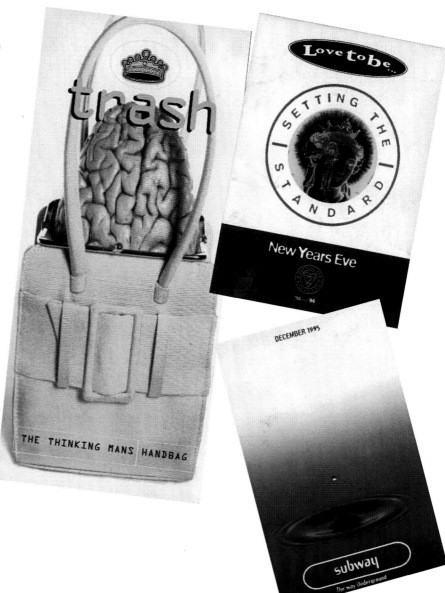

Inside the Niche publicity office

Partying in the City Hall ballroom

A visit to Club Uropa

The legendary 'Dirty Stop Out's Tour' wasn't for the faint-hearted

Outside the Rhythm Room on a busy Saturday night

END OF AN ERA THAT WILL NEVER BE REPEATED

The 1990s witnessed the rise and fall of Sheffield as a leading UK party destination.

The growth was unprecedented but the cracks were beginning to appear long before the Millennium as late bars like the Casbah started to introduce fierce new competition for established nightclubs and the bottom was falling out of the dance market nationally.

Though nightclubs remain today, the stranglehold they once had over the after dark scene is now largely consigned to history.

Have things improved for the better? Well the move towards round the clock licensing was modelled in part on the drinking attitudes of key European countries; places like France where a relaxed glass of wine could last all evening and binge drinking was largely unheard of.

The speed and quantity drunk in Blighty remains largely unchanged - it's just the time of night that people concentrate their efforts that has changed.

People go out far later and cheap booze from supermarkets is consumed at home by the bucketload to avoid paying the higher prices in clubs and bars.

It will be interesting to see how people are describing the noughties in a decade or so's time.

But for now, we'll leave you with the kind of nightclub choice you'd have been faced with when you stepped out the door in the winter of 1995; when house music was at its height, when Pulp (and more than a few others) were 'Sorted for E's and Wizz' and nightclub owners had to charge a king's ransom to get in their club because people were swapping alcohol for water and the DJs were costing a small fortune.

We'd lost one of our most iconic clubs, The Limit, which bowed out in 1991 and the venue the management took over, the Palais, had now metamorphosized into the thriving Music Factory.

The London Road operation was largely seen as catalyst for starting to put Sheffield in the premier league of '90s clubbing venues.

Saturday's 'Love to be...' was a true phenomenon with queues forming long before doors opened and coaches turned up from here, there and everywhere to hear the likes of Boy George, Danny Rampling, Pete Tong and others spinning the discs.

Friday's 'Steel', promoted by Leeds clubbing outfit 'Up Yer Ronson', offered DJ glitterati like Graeme Park, Sasha, Jeremy Healey and Brandon Block.

Far more out of sight, but no less influential, was Walker Street's Arches venue - sitting under the Victorian railway arches of the Wicker.

The 650 capacity venue truly felt underground. The parents were never going to find you here amongst

the down-at-heel backstreets awash with takeaway blight and black cabs.

Uncompromising, non-commercial house was the make up of Saturday's flagship 'Subway' event with standard-bearing DJs of the era

like Paul Oakenfold, Danny Rampling and John Digweed at the helm.

Far more unassuming was Carver Street's Beluga. The small, downstairs venue generally minded its own business, kept out of the media and entertained its loyal crowd.

Its outlook was mainstream, sensible and it seemed a pretty model citizen as far as after dark venues went.

The sprawling Roxy did what it had been doing since it opened in the mid-1980s - being big, brash and regularly entertaining 7,000 punters in a single week.

Many referred to it as a cattle market on a weekend, they weren't far wrong. But it had a diehard following. One recent reunion sold out at a drop of a hat!

But it did far more than mainstream chart weekends. It had a thriving rock night, student night, over 25s night and more.

Niche was an enigma. The 200 capacity venue didn't open until midnight, didn't serve alcohol and kicked out at 8am. It was only in its infancy at this stage. Its music policy was garage, house, funky beats and dance courtesy of resident DJs Daz Wilkes and Paul Revere.

Though Josephines would be saying thank you and good night by the Millennium, the venue that originally opened in 1976 was still going strong in 1995.

It was riding high following it being awarded the Molson Beda Disco of the Year Award for the North of England.

No other nightclub offered catering or an experience like it. It's a la

ORCHIS

"Sheffield's finest club venue"

Orchis · 24 Carver Street · Sheffield
tel 0114 273 8677

carte restaurant offered some of the best food in the city and tables were regularly booked up weeks in advance.

Dress codes were ultra-strict and the traditional values were overseen by its owner; one of Sheffield's most successful businessmen, leisure boss Dave Allen.

The 1990s were a halcyon period for the Leadmill. The venue could hardly put a foot wrong. Club nights, band nights - things seemed to be working like a dream. The venue that was born out of left leaning values even ran one of the city's most successful house nights, Friday's 'Rise'.

It's club night roster was the envy of much of the city's after dark scene; 'La Videotech' '80s night, Thursday's 'Beat Club' and Saturday night indie soiree, 'Joyrider'.

Add to that its groundbreaking gig line-up and it was a true after dark force to be reckoned with.

In fact it was so successful it even ran out of space for its growing roster of club nights.

'70s disco had a massive resurgence in the 1990s and things

didn't come much better than the Leadmill's 'Hotpants' night that was a regular visitor to the City Hall Ballroom in the era.

The night was a sea of gaudy afro wigs, larger than life lapels, unfeasibly large, billowing trousers and the coolest tunes.

The Leadmill also installed 'Step On' indie night whilst DJs Mike Bottomly, Gaz Snowden and Mutley fired up 'Drop' on the first three Friday nights each month.

Though Cairos would eventually bow out, in 1995 it was still packing them in. The massive Bank Street club was shamelessly mainstream and kitted out in the spirit of Tutankhamun (or maybe more like Tutankhamun after he'd consumed a lot of spirits). Six bars, diner and Silks pub next door.

Matilda Street's Capitol arrived at the expense of legendary rock club, Rebels. In the days when new licenses were few and far between, the only way to open a new venue seemed to be via the transference of permissions from another venue.

So Rebels was shut and the alcohol licence switched to the glitzy new Capitol.

Rock music was part of the initial mix but it was soon surplus to requirements as dance nights like Saturday's 'Forbidden Fruit' took over.

Club Uropa, formerly Isabella's, was also a formidable operation. They'd got their own Molson Beda Award for the best new nightclub under 1000 capacity, as well as the adjoining Berlins fun pub.

The Eyre Street operation was on its ascendancy and would soon be helping launch Viva Salsa Latin night which added a further dimension to the city's offering.

Kikis was cool, kitsch and voted one of the best venues in the UK by readers of style mag, The Face.

It was renowned as the home of 'Trash', the midweek, gay/straight, dance/disco, palatial cross-dressing extravaganza.

The Charter Square venue also held Friday's 'Kitten Club' and Saturday's 'Wonderland' - again,

both dance orientated.

It also boasted sister venue, Cuba. The 200 capacity venue was probably best known for much of the 1990s as the home of 'Reservoir Rocks', the metal night that provided a home for the rockers following the demise of Rebels.

The Republic needs little introduction and arrived towards the end of the year.

Last but not least was the outings offered by the two universities.

Hallam's 'Sheff 1' was celebrating a decade of student mayhem whilst Friday's 'Stardust' walked the '70s and '80s retro trail.

Western Bank's Sheffield University was renowned for its Saturday night 'Pop Tarts' retro night and regular Friday gay outing, Climax.

Club promoter Dean Longden

**Enjoying a night
on the tiles**

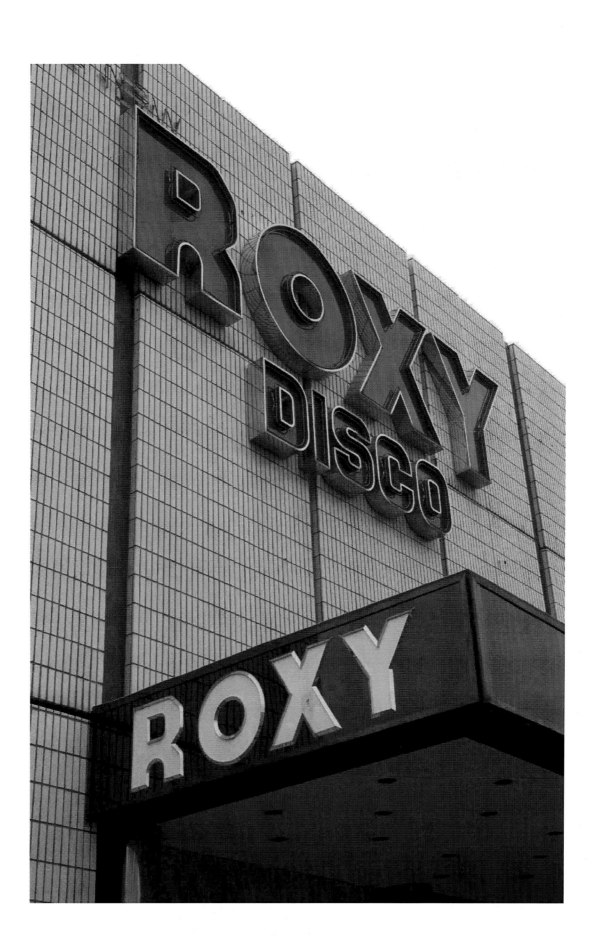

The last night of the legendary Limit in 1991

Clubbing couple Coronation Street actress Chloe Newsome and Fabrice Limon

Casbah DJs Detox and Rat

The author

Neil Anderson

Neil Anderson first launched Sheffield's 'Dirty Stop Out's Guide(TM)' in 1995 as a no-holds barred insight into the city's after dark scene.

He went retro with the 'Dirty Stop Out's Guide To 1970s Sheffield' in 2010 and followed that, more recently, with '50s, 60s and '80s versions.

It's fair to say, doing the '90s version makes him feel extremely old but also extremely grateful to have been a part of one of the most vibrant periods in the city's after dark history.

Neil Anderson has written on nightlife and entertainment for titles spanning The Independent to The Big Issue and was a Sheffield Telegraph columnist for 12 years.

When he's not writing books he's busy publishing them through acmretro.com or promoting them and other businesses through neilandersonmedia.com.

Acknowledgements

Sheffield Newspapers for use of their wonderful pictures and Sheffield Telegraph for accommodating the 'Dirty Stop Out's' column for over a decade, Neil Midgley, Colin Drury, Andy Barker, Chris Calow, Phil Staniland, Karl Lang, Steve Stevlor, Richard Abbey, Stephanie Del'Nero, Steve Bush, Laura Hayes, David Dunn, John Quinn, Mark Sheridan, Alex Usbourne, Jamie Headcharge, Bob Worm, Jill Theobald, Garry Wilson and Simon Mander.

All round inspiration: Lindsay McLaren.

Proofing: Peter Eales.

Balancing the books: Ian Cheetham.

Layout: Karen Davies.

Cover: Carl Flint (www.carlflint.com)

Dedicated to Lowri, Ewan and Dylan Anderson.

The Dirty Stop Out's Guide trademark is owned by Neil Anderson and licensed to ACM Retro Ltd.

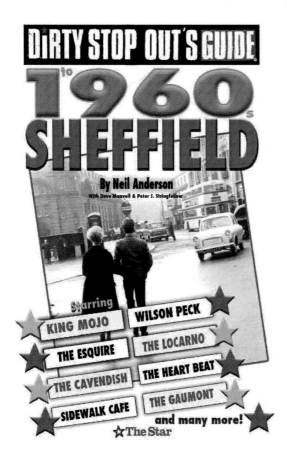

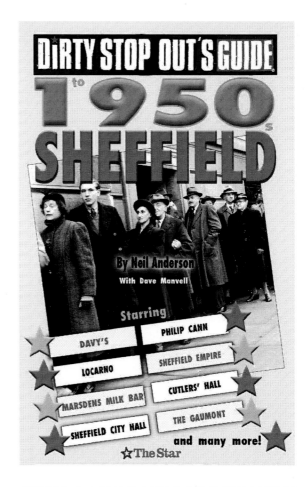